Shine Your Light:
A Kid's Guide to Reiki Healing

April D'Amato

Shine Your Light:
A Kid's Guide to Reiki Healing

April D'Amato

Soul Star Healing
2019

First Printing: 2019
ISBN: 978-0-578-42164-3

To order this book, contact:
April D'Amato
april@soulstarhealing.com

Soul Star Healing
P.O. Box 1404
Guilford CT 06437
www.soulstarhealing.com

Dedication

To the New Children who have come to this planet to assist humanity with its great shift in human consciousness. They have come here to truly show us the way: to shed light on what is not working, to prompt us to make changes individually as well as globally, to challenge our beliefs and expectations, to defy our limitations and to expand our consciousness beyond duality and separation.

Thank you. With the help of these children, we will embrace a new direction on earth, one that includes peace, harmony and unity.

Table of Contents

Acknowledgements

I would like to thank the Archangels, my Spirit Guides and Galactic Team for helping me to create not only a class that embraces the sensitivities of these beautiful new children to our planet, but to write this book. I thank the Earth Angels, my friends, family and students of Reiki for their love, support and faith in me. I extend a huge thank you to Susannah MacNeil for her endless patience, support and expert editing skills. Without Susannah, you would not be reading this right now. Finally, and most importantly, thank you Kate Clancy of Kelana Design, the masterful artist who not only created the cover of the book but also made the illustrations to make this book into a usable workbook for children.

Preface

I named this book "Shine Your Light" because I encourage you to be and express who you are. The "light" is the love you already have inside of you.

Over my years as an intuitive and healer, I have found that one of the best ways to keep your light shining is through Reiki. Reiki is a form of Energy Healing, and one of the many tools you can use to shine your light. Your job here, as a human being, on Earth is to shine so brightly that the love you have and share will help the Earth and all the living beings on the planet.

I worked with the Angels to develop this manual after teaching Reiki to children for several years. It is meant to accompany my classes and any class that is teaching children Reiki. I found that when I taught Reiki to children and adults, I often discussed self awareness, self love and self care as well as Reiki. This workbook is not only for learning Reiki, but it is also designed to help you learn a little more about you and how you can maintain your wellness. I hope this guide will help you begin or a continue your journey in shining your light.

This is a poem that I channeled from the Angels specifically to be shared in this book.

Shine. Shine. Shine.
It is time. It is time.
The Earth needs your light to shine.
Don't be afraid of a new day.
It's all in your power to make it your way.
Angels, Spirits and guides from above
Are all here to show you how to use your light to love.
Your light is the gift you can give.
Simply choose to be happy and show it as you live.
Shine. Shine. Shine.
It is time. It is time.
The Earth needs your light to shine.

In love and light,
April

Shine Your Light:
A Kid's Guide to Reiki Healing

April D'Amato

What Is Energy?

Energy is also known as life force energy. It has been called by different names, including Ki, Prana and Chi. Every living thing contains this life force energy. It is what makes us alive.

What Is Energy? *continued*

It's in people!

And it's in you too!

If We Can't See Energy, How Do We Know It's There?

Energy is all around us.

To most people energy is invisible, but some people can see it. Energy is something you can practice seeing. Just because you don't see it doesn't mean it isn't there. Your radio and mobile phone use energy and act as receivers of energy. We can't see the radio waves, or the cellular tower transmission, but we know that they work because you are able to listen to the radio and answer your cell phone.

A good thing to remember is that all energy needs both a sender and a receiver for the connection to work.

Feeling Energy: The Energy Ball

One way to sense energy is to feel it.

Put your hands together and pull them about four inches apart. Do you notice anything?

Now, try imagining a ball of energy between your palms—it would be look like a glowing ball of light. Do you feel anything?

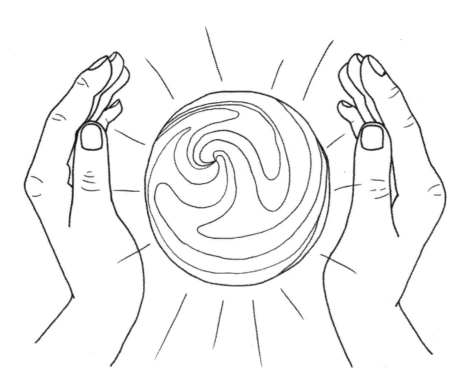

F ... l *continued*

S| ...all as if you are shaping it like a ball of clay or just
fe| ...your hands closer together and then apart. Do you
fe| ...and pull your hands together? You might even be able
to| ...practice this exercise, the more you will experience it.

Feeling Energy: The Pendulum

Another way you can sense your energy is using a pendulum. A pendulum is something you create with a string and a weight on one end. The most important thing is that it needs to be able to swing freely.

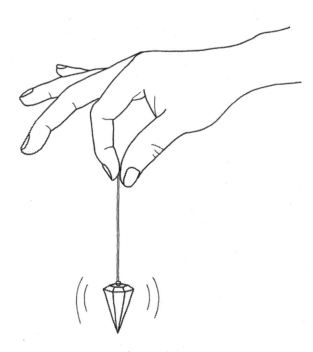

You can make your own pendulum with a button and a string

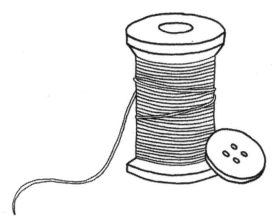

What Is an Aura?

An aura is what we call the energy field around your body.   Everyone and everything has an aura: even your animal friends and plants too!   We can get to know the aura through all of our senses.   When we learn Reiki, we will begin to sense the aura in a number of ways.   In this chapter, we will practice sensing the aura with our eyes, ears and hands.

Label the aura layers.

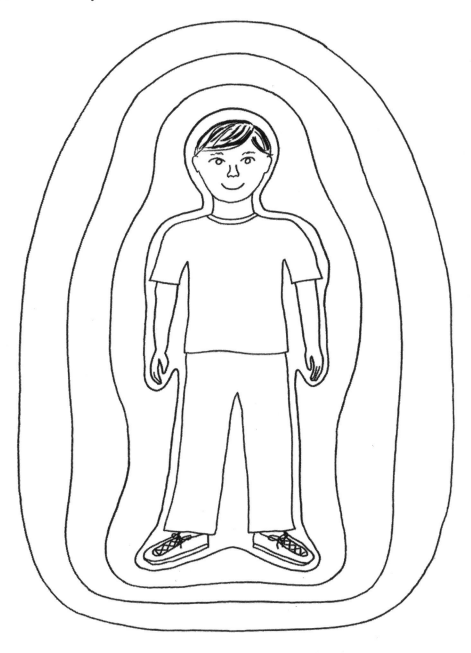

Aura Layers

The aura has four layers. The following are the names of the aura layers:

- ◆ Physical- this is the layer closest to the physical body.
- ◆ Emotional-this is made up of our emotions/feelings.
- ◆ Mental- this layer is made up of our thoughts.
- ◆ Spiritual- this is our connection to our higher or spiritual self.

How big do you think your aura is?

Aura Colors

Everyone's aura has a unique energetic imprint just like a fingerprint. It varies in shapes, sizes and colors. Our aura is a made up of a vibration, therefore, it is constantly moving and continuously changing based upon our surroundings and our experiences. This vibration can often be seen by people as a color. The aura is greatly influenced by the energy centers in our body, called chakras.

What color do you think your aura is? Is it more than one color?

Say your name out loud…what color comes to mind when you say your name? Could that be the color of your aura?

What Are Chakras?

Chakras are energy centers located in the body. The Sanskrit word, *"chakra"* means "wheel" or "disk" because each chakra moves with a spinning motion. There are seven major physical chakras in our bodies. They are located at the top of the head, and down along your spine finishing at the base of your spine. Each chakra has a color and certain characteristics associated with it.

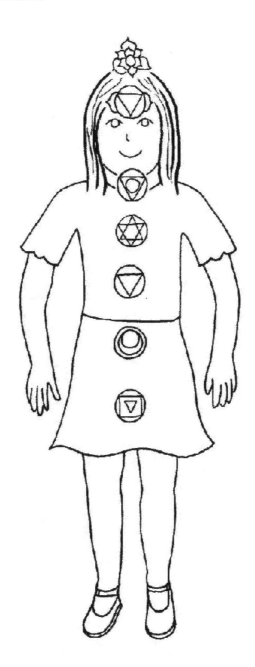

Seven Chakras

1. Root Chakra

The *root chakra* center is located at the base of your spine. The energy here is all about you and your family, where you live and your culture. It is also your connection to the Earth.

Questions to think about:

Who is in your family?

What are some special traditions of your family?

Did you know that all people of the Earth are also part of your family?

2. Sacral Chakra

The *sacral chakra* is in your belly. This is where you hold all your feelings: happy, sad or mad. Even confused and silly too!! This chakra holds all the feelings that you have for other people as well as for yourself. It is also where you find your creative energy.

Questions to think about:

Do you know how it feels to feel happy or sad?

Do you do a creative hobby?

Did you know that sometimes when you have a tummy ache it can be caused by a feeling that is stuck in this energy center?

Seven Chakras *continued*

3. Solar Plexus Chakra

The *solar plexus chakra* is located just above your belly-button. It is where you learn to say yes and no. This is where you learn to make a decision about what you want. For example: do you want to go outside and play or stay in and read a book? Sometimes you may say or do things that you feel bad about later; this is where you think about it.

Questions to think about:
How do you feel when you tell someone yes you will do something when you mean to say no?

Do you ever have trouble deciding what you want to wear or deciding what to eat for a snack?

4. Heart Chakra

The *heart chakra* is located in the middle of your chest next to your real heart. It is all about loving yourself, just as you are. It also reminds you to tell the people you love that you love them. And it is the place where we do our healing.

Questions to think about:

How can you love yourself more?

Who do you love, but sometimes forget to tell?

5. Throat Chakra

The *throat chakra* is in your throat. It helps you express who you are by using your voice. You sing, laugh, talk and speak your feelings from this chakra. It is always important to say what you are feeling and thinking as long as you are speaking from your heart and not in an angry mood.

Questions to think about:

What is your favorite song to sing?

What makes you laugh?

6. Brow Chakra

The *brow chakra* is also called the *third eye*. If you had an actual third eye, where do you think it would be? That is exactly where this energy center is located. What do you think it would look like? This is where your sixth sense, intuitive sense, is located. (We will talk more about this a little later.)

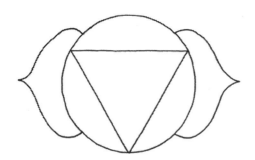

Questions to think about:

Do you ever think of someone and then they call you?

Do you ever dream of something and then it comes true?

Seven Chakras *continued*

7. Crown Chakra

The *crown chakra* is located on top of your head. It is the highest point on your body. This is where you connect to the sky, heaven and God.

Questions to think about:

Do you have a favorite prayer you say before you go to bed?

Do you have a special place where you like to pray?

What do the colors of the Chakras remind you of?

Senses

What Are the Senses?

The senses are parts of our body that provide us with information about the world around us.
We have five physical senses: hearing, sight, touch, smell and taste.
Can you identify them in the pictures below?

_____   _____

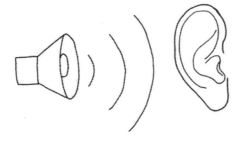

_____

_____   _____

The Sixth Sense

Did you know that we actually have *six senses*? Sometimes we forget to teach about our Sixth Sense; but we all have it!

The sixth sense is also called our intuitive sense. It is not a physical sense and it is not something you can see with your eyes. Have you ever just known and understood that something was true, even if grown-ups don't recognize it? When you "just know" information is real because your heart knows it to be true, that is your sixth sense at work.

Everyone is born with the sixth sense, but not everyone uses it or practices it. Everyone experiences intuition differently. Sometimes, it may make you feel happy, and sometimes it may make you feel uncomfortable. Here are some examples of your sixth sense at work:

- Butterflies in your tummy.
- A tingly feeling when you are talking about something.
- Seeing things in your dreams.
- Hearing an angel speak to you.
- Just knowing something.

When we listen with more than our ears, when we see with more than our eyes, and when we truly feel from our hearts, we can learn what our intuition is telling us. The more you pay attention, the more you will experience the magic of the sixth sense. It is magical because not everyone pays attention to it, but those of us who do are pretty special! Intuition can be a very helpful guide as we go through life.

What Are Feelings?

Feelings are how we express our emotions.

We are made up of a rainbow of emotions. Your feelings make you aware of how an action, thought or thing affects you. If your emotions are a rainbow, what does your rainbow look like right now? Draw it here.

The Role of Feelings

Feelings play a large role in our lives. They tell us a lot about what is happening around us. But not all feelings feel good. On our journey of growing up, we don't always feel happy. Sometimes things happen that make us sad, mad, confused or embarrassed--and that's okay. We are supposed to feel all of our feelings--that is why we have them.

If you allow yourself to feel all of your emotions, it's easier to be who you are. By learning to identify what makes you feel each of those feelings, you can learn to change them and help yourself to feel better.

Name some of the feelings you feel often.

Do you find it hard to express your feelings? Do you trust your feelings to help you know what to do? How do you feel today?

What Makes You Feel?

What things make you feel sad? Make a list below of four things that make you feel sad.

What helps you feel better when you are sad? Write your own ideas below. If you learned something new in class, include the new ideas too!

What Makes You Feel? *continued*

What things make you feel embarrassed? Make a list below of four things that make you feel embarrassed.

What helps you feel better when you are embarrassed? Write your own ideas below. If you learned something new in class, include the new ideas too!

What Makes You Feel? *continued*

What things make you feel confused? Make a list below of four things that make you feel confused.

What helps you feel better when you are confused? Write your own ideas below. If you learned something new in class, include the new ideas too!

What Makes You Feel? *continued*

What things make you feel mad? Make a list below of four things that make you feel mad.

What helps you feel better when you are mad? Write your own ideas below. If you learned something new in class, include the new ideas too!

How to Feel Better

Now that you know what brings on your feelings, let's talk about how to change those feelings. Reiki is one way to help with that, but there are other ways too! You can use breathing, singing, moving, laughing or silliness to change your energy and feel good again.

Laughter is a great way to change an unhappy feeling to a happy one. What things do you do that make you feel happy or silly or make you laugh?   Write a list below.

How to Feel Better *continued*

The most important thing to remember is who we are and where we come from. We are love, and we come from love. But you may wonder, "How can I remember that when I'm not *feeling* any love?" The answer is that *you can learn to move your energy, thoughts and feelings to a place of love.* One way to start is to think about the things you like.

Use the space below to list the things that make your spirit happy. The next time you are feeling down, review this list and do the things that make you feel better. That way, you can actually move yourself back to a place of love.

Ways to Care for Yourself

Reiki has amazing healing powers, but it works better when you combine it with other healthy activities. Here are some things you can do to make Reiki work better.

- Eat healthy foods. (lots of vegetables and fruits)

- Drink lots of water.

- Move your body. (exercise)
- Get plenty of sleep.
- Spend time outside.

Ways to Care for Yourself *continued*

- Talk about your feelings.
- Develop an attitude of gratitude--be thankful for the good things in your life.
- Think happy thoughts.
- Create your own affirmation (positive statement) here.

Ways to Care for Yourself *continued*

Listen to Your Body

Your body is amazing--it can do so many things! It can even heal itself. Remember the last time you cut your finger or scraped your knee? You probably didn't have to go to the doctor to make it feel better. That's because your body can heal itself.

Your body works hard to keep you feeling good, but sometimes something causes your body not to work as well. We call this *disease or illness*. When you think about it, *disease* is "dis-ease"--the opposite of being at ease. *Ease* means it is easy for your body to do its day-to-day functions and heal itself; when it is not easy, that is how disease occurs. Holding in your feelings, not sleeping enough, living in a polluted or noisy environment, having poor nutrition, and other bad things can cause disease.

Your body will always let you know when something doesn't feel good, and it's really important to listen to those signs. By paying attention to the messages from your body, you can often find a way to heal or prevent it from getting dis-ease.

What kinds of signs might your body give you that you are not well? List your ideas below.

If your body is telling you what you aren't well, what can you do about it? List your ideas below.

Grounding

Grounding is the practice of connecting yourself to the core of the Earth. We feel healthier and happier when our energy is balanced--and grounding is one of the best ways to do that. It is also a great help when you are doing Reiki. You should ground your energy every day.

There are many ways to ground your energy. Below are some examples to choose from.

To begin, it helps to visualize yourself as a beautiful tree with leaves and flowers or fruits growing on the branches.

1. Find a comfortable spot indoors or outdoors. Now imagine you have roots (like tree roots) coming out of the bottoms of your feet growing down into the core of Earth. Then imagine, Mother Earth sending beautiful love energy up into your roots, while brilliant white light pours into your crown (the top of your head) from above.

2. Find a comfortable spot indoors or outdoors. Sit cross-legged. Now send a light beam from the base of your spine (your root chakra) into the core of the Earth. Imagine, Mother Earth sending beautiful love energy up into your roots while brilliant white light pours into your crown (the top of your head) from a giant sun above you.

3. Find a tree outside. You can hug the tree or just sit down in front of it with your back against the tree trunk. Either way, imagine, Mother Earth sending beautiful love energy up into your roots through your feet or the base of your spine (your root chakra) while brilliant white light pours into your crown (the top of your head) from above.

4. Find a comfortable spot indoors or outdoors, and sit or stand. Close your eyes, visualize yourself as a tall, majestic tree. Imagine that your feet are the tops of the roots and your body is the tree trunk. Now lift your arms up and out as if they are branches. Take the time to imagine the leaves growing on the tree, and imagine flowers or fruits growing on the branches. Once you "see" the flower or fruits, you'll know that you have grounded.

What Is Reiki?

Reiki is a Japanese word to describe a type of energy healing, and it's what you are learning in this book.

In Japanese, the word *Reiki* looks like this:

When you say the word *Reiki,* it sounds like this:

"Rei"   "ki"

What Does *Reiki* Mean?

Translated from Japanese to English, *Reiki* means "guided life force energy".

The essence of Reiki is love, peace, harmony, cooperation and trust. When you do Reiki on yourself or others you give a gift of healing and love. Healing energy flows automatically to where it is needed and works on all the layers of the aura. As you do Reiki, you become a connector for the life force energy. You can act as both the sender and the receiver.

The History of Reiki

Mikao Usui was the man who rediscovered the ancient healing art of Reiki. He always wanted to help people. When Usui grew up he became a doctor. He wanted people to live full, healthy and balanced lives so he sought out to learn the ancient healing secrets. He spoke to many wise older people, known as "elders" trying to find answers to his questions. Many people told him that he would never be able to discover the secrets because they were lost to our world. But Usui was not discouraged; he believed in his dream of helping people.

Instead of giving up he studied ancient writings that contained secrets of living and healing-- and he learned that--in order to, heal others, he must first heal himself. Usui went on a 21-day retreat to the Holy Mountain of Kurama where he spent his time fasting and meditating (quieting his mind). Usui gathered 21 stones to keep track of his time on the mountain; each day he threw one away. On the 21st day, he connected with the system of energy healing known as Reiki. He received information on the ancient symbols and how to use them.

After his retreat, Usui went home and practiced using what he learned. He found that Reiki really worked, and he shared it with other people he wanted to help. While Usui was alive he taught Reiki to other teachers so that the world would never again be without this ancient healing art. Today, there are thousands of Reiki Masters who teach Reiki all over the world. You are learning from me, and I am one of those Reiki Masters!

Reiki Attunement

The Reiki Attunement is a special process that allows a Reiki Master to connect the Reiki energy to his or her student. It activates your inner ability to heal. It puts Reiki energy into your hands so that you can give other people energy without losing any of your own energy.

Reiki attunement makes it possible to "turn on" Reiki energy just by thinking about it. You may notice that your hands are heating up. That's Reiki at work!

Remember to use Reiki whenever you need a little extra love, or you want to give out a little extra love. It will help you to feel calm, relaxed and happier.

Using Reiki

Reiki can be used for everything! You can use it on yourself or on other people, plants or animals. It is a wonderful tool that can be used to help all living things. And, once you have learned Reiki, you will always have it. It will be there for you for the rest of your life.

You can Reiki your animal friends.

Using Reiki *continued*

You can even do Reiki on *yourself!* You can do Reiki every day to keep your attitude happy and your physical body healthy.

You can use Reiki for anything and everything you can think of. You can use it to help when you have difficulty going to sleep because you are worried. You can use it when you feel nervous.

You can use it to get focused when doing your homework or studying for a test. You can even use it to help yourself feel better when you are sick.

Afterword

Now that you have completed the Reiki training, you are considered a Reiki Practitioner. That's a fancy way of saying you can now do Reiki on yourself as well as others! *Practice* is the best advice I can give to you about what to do next. *Practice. Practice. Practice.* The more you practice Reiki on yourself and others in your day-to-day life, the stronger your connection will be to Reiki and your Sixth Sense.

Finally, the best thing about Reiki is that you can never leave home without it, because it's right there inside of you! It will never disappear. You may forget that you have been attuned to Reiki, but it never forgets you. This is a gift that will last your entire life.

This is just the beginning of your lifelong journey to self-healing and empowerment.

Made in the USA
Monee, IL
19 July 2021